DEBT-FREE

*A step by step guide to
financial freedom*

Summary

The book "Debt-Free" A step-by-step guide to achieving

financial freedom. The book begins by explaining the snowball effect taught by Dave Ramsey and its benefits and then moves on to assessing your current debt situation. In Lesson 3, the book provides guidance on creating a debt repayment plan, including prioritizing debts and adjusting your budget. Finally, Lesson 4 explains how to utilize your home equity to accelerate debt repayment. With practical advice and actionable steps, this book is a valuable resource for anyone looking to take control of their finances and become debt-free.In Lesson 5 of "Becoming Debt-Free," readers learn how to stay on track and motivated during the debt repayment process. The book offers tips for reducing expenses and increasing income, as well as strategies for celebrating progress and staying committed to becoming debt-free. Lesson 6 focuses on finding purpose to keep readers motivated throughout their journey. By answering a series of questions related to family, children, and retirement, readers can identify a purpose that will drive their efforts towards financial freedom. With practical advice and actionable steps, this book is a valuable resource for anyone looking to take control of their finances and become debt-free

TABLE OF CONTENTS

Lesson 1: Understanding the Snowball Effect and Its Benefits

- *What is the snowball effect?*
- *Why is the snowball effect an effective strategy for becoming debt-free?*
- *How can the snowball effect help you pay off your mortgage and other debts faster?*

Lesson 2: Assessing Your Current Debt Situation

- *How much debt do you currently have?*
- *What types of debt do you have and what are the interest rates?*
- *What is your current monthly payment on each debt?*
- *How much equity do you have in your home?*

Lesson 3: Creating a Debt Repayment Plan

- *How to prioritize your debts for repayment using the snowball effect*
- *How to allocate funds towards your debt payments*
- *How to adjust your budget to maximize your debt repayment*

Lesson 4: Utilizing Your Home Equity

to Accelerate Debt Repayment

- *What is home equity and how does it work?*
- *How to access your home equity to pay off debt faster*
- *Pros and cons of using home equity for debt repayment*

Lesson 5: Staying on Track and Motivated

- *How to stay motivated during the debt repayment process*
- *Tips for reducing expenses and increasing income*
- *How to celebrate your progress and stay committed to becoming debt-free*

Lesson 6: Finding your purpose to keep you motivated.

In this lesson we'll identify several ways to find purpose to motivate you. You'll be asked a series of questions to trigger your mind to start thinking the right way. Your debt isn't just your problem.

Lesson 7: Its a Marathon, not a sprint!

Course review reviewing everything we went over. And reminding you to take it one day at a time. Becoming debt free is not going to happen over night.

This course would include lessons, and potentially additional resources such as worksheets to help you apply the concepts to your specific financial situation.

LESSON 1: UNDERSTANDING THE SNOWBALL EFFECT AND ITS BENEFITS

Welcome to this course on using the snowball effect to become debt-free using your mortgage and equity in your home. In this lesson, we will introduce you to the snowball effect and why it is an effective strategy for becoming debt-free.

What is the snowball effect?

The snowball effect is a debt repayment strategy that involves paying off your debts in order of smallest to largest, regardless of interest rates. This strategy is taugh by financial expert Dave Ramsey. We've modified it for simplicity. You start by making minimum payments on all of your debts except for the smallest one. You then put as much money as possible towards paying off the smallest debt until it is completely paid off. Once the smallest debt is paid off, you move on to the next smallest debt and repeat the process until all of your debts are paid off.

The snowball effect gets its name from the way that the amount of money you can put towards your debts grows like a snowball as you pay off each debt. By focusing on paying off the smallest debt first, you build momentum and motivation to continue paying off your other debts.

Why is the snowball effect an effective strategy for becoming debt-free?

The snowball effect is an effective strategy for becoming debt-free because it helps you to quickly eliminate some of your debts, which can help to reduce your overall debt burden. When you pay off a debt, you no longer have to make monthly payments towards it, which frees up more money to put towards your other debts. This can help you to pay off your other debts faster, resulting in a snowball effect where you are able to pay off all of your debts more quickly than if you were simply making minimum payments on all of your debts.

Additionally, the snowball effect can be psychologically motivating. Paying off debt can be a long and challenging process, and it can be easy to become discouraged if you don't see progress quickly. By focusing on paying off the smallest debts first, you can see progress more quickly, which can help you to stay motivated and committed to the debt repayment process.

How can the snowball effect help you pay off your mortgage and other debts faster?

The snowball effect can be used to pay off any type of debt, including your mortgage. If you have other debts in addition to your mortgage, such as credit card debt or car loans, you can use the snowball effect to pay off those debts first. Once those debts are paid off, you can then put the money you were using to pay off those debts towards paying off your mortgage faster.

Using your home equity can also be a powerful tool in this process. By accessing your home equity, you can use that money to pay off high-interest debts, which can help you to pay off your debts more quickly. With fewer debts to pay off, you can then put more money towards paying off your mortgage, which can help you to become debt-free faster.

In summary, the snowball effect is a powerful debt repayment strategy that can help you to become debt-free faster. By focusing on paying off your smallest debts first, you can build momentum and motivation to continue paying off your other debts. This strategy can be used to pay off any type of debt, including your mortgage, and can be combined with accessing your home equity to accelerate your debt repayment.

LESSON 2: ASSESSING YOUR CURRENT DEBT SITUATION

Welcome to Lesson 2 of this course on using the snowball effect to become debt-free using your mortgage and equity in your home. In this lesson, we will discuss how to assess your current debt situation.

How much debt do you currently have?

The first step in assessing your debt situation is to determine how much debt you currently have. Make a list of all your debts, including credit card debt, car loans, student loans, personal loans, and your mortgage. Include the name of the creditor, the balance owed, and the interest rate for each debt.

What types of debt do you have and what are the interest rates?

Once you have a list of your debts, the next step is to determine the type of debt and the interest rate for each debt. This will help you to prioritize which debts to pay off first using the snowball effect. Typically, you will want to focus on paying off debts with the highest interest rates first, as these debts will cost you the most money in interest over time.

What is your current monthly payment on each debt?

In addition to knowing the balance and interest rate for each debt, it is important to know your current monthly payment on each debt. This will help you to determine how much money you can put towards paying off your debts using the snowball effect.

How much equity do you have in your home?

Finally, it is important to determine how much equity you have in your home. Home equity is the difference between the current market value of your home and the amount you owe on your mortgage. To calculate your home equity, subtract your mortgage balance from the current market value of your home. For example, if your home is worth $300,000 and you owe $200,000 on your mortgage, your home equity is $100,000.

Knowing your home equity is important because it can be used to accelerate your debt repayment using the snowball effect. By accessing your home equity, you can use that money to pay off high-interest debts, which can help you to pay off your debts more quickly. With fewer debts to pay off, you can then put more money towards paying off your mortgage, which can help you to become debt-free faster.

In summary, assessing your current debt situation is an important step in using the snowball effect to become debt-free using your mortgage and equity in your home. By determining how much debt you have, the type of debt and interest rate for each debt, your current monthly payment on each debt, and your home equity, you can create a plan for paying off your debts and becoming debt-free more quickly.

LESSON 3: CREATING A DEBT REPAYMENT PLAN

Welcome to Lesson 3 of this course on using the snowball effect to become debt-free using your mortgage and equity in your home. In this lesson, we will discuss how to create a debt repayment plan using the snowball effect.

How to prioritize your debts for repayment using the snowball effect

The first step in creating a debt repayment plan using the snowball effect is to prioritize your debts for repayment. You should start by paying off your smallest debt first, regardless of the interest rate. Once that debt is paid off, you can then move on to the next smallest debt and repeat the process until all of your debts are paid off.

Paying off your smallest debt first can help to build momentum and motivation to continue paying off your other debts. Once you have paid off your smallest debt, you will have one less debt to worry about and can put the money you were using to pay off that debt towards paying off your other debts.

How to allocate funds towards your debt payments

Once you have prioritized your debts for repayment using the snowball effect, the next step is to allocate funds towards your debt payments. You should start by making the minimum payments on all of your debts except for the smallest one. You should then put as much money as possible towards paying off the smallest debt.

Once the smallest debt is paid off, you can then move on to the next smallest debt and repeat the process. As you pay off each debt, you will have more money available to put towards paying off your other debts, which will help you to pay off your debts more quickly.

How to adjust your budget to maximize your debt repayment

In order to maximize your debt repayment using the snowball effect, you may need to adjust your budget. This may involve cutting back on discretionary spending, such as eating out or going on vacations, in order to free up more money to put towards paying off your debts.

You may also want to consider increasing your income by taking on a side job or selling items you no longer need. By increasing your income, you will have more money available to put towards paying off your debts, which can help you to pay off your debts more quickly.

In summary, creating a debt repayment plan using the snowball effect involves prioritizing your debts for repayment, allocating funds towards your debt payments, and adjusting your budget to maximize your debt repayment. By following these steps, you can create a plan for paying off your debts and becoming debt-free more quickly.

PAY OFF DEBTS

LESSON 4: UTILIZING YOUR HOME EQUITY TO ACCELERATE DEBT REPAYMENT

When it comes to paying off debt, there are a variety of strategies you can use to make progress and ultimately achieve financial freedom. One strategy that some homeowners use is utilizing their home equity to pay off debt faster. In this lesson, we will explore the concept of home equity, how it works, and the pros and cons of using it to accelerate debt repayment.

What is Home Equity and How Does it Work?

Home equity is the difference between the current market value of your home and the amount you still owe on your mortgage. For example, if your home is currently worth $300,000 and you still owe $200,000 on your mortgage, you have $100,000 in home equity.

Home equity can increase in two ways: either by paying down your mortgage or by the market value of your home appreciating. Over time, as you continue to make your mortgage payments, the amount of equity you have in your home will typically increase.

How to Access Your Home Equity to Pay Off Debt Faster

There are two primary ways to access your home equity to pay off debt faster: a home equity loan/home equity line of credit (HELOC) or a cash out refinance.

A home equity loan is a lump sum loan that is secured by your home equity. You receive the funds as a one-time payment and then make regular payments to pay it back, typically over a period of 5-15 years. The interest rate on a home equity loan is typically fixed, meaning it doesn't change over the life of the loan.

A HELOC, on the other hand, is a revolving line of credit that is also secured by your home equity. You can borrow as much or as little as you need, up to a certain limit, and you only pay interest on the amount you borrow. The interest rate on a HELOC is typically variable, meaning it can change over time.

A cash-out refinance is a financial strategy that involves refinancing your existing mortgage for a higher amount than what you currently owe and then using the difference in cash to pay off other debts. This strategy can be a powerful tool to accelerate your journey towards becoming debt-free.

One of the primary benefits of a cash-out refinance is that it can help you consolidate high-interest debt into a lower interest rate mortgage loan. For example, if you have credit card debt with interest rates of 20% or more, a cash-out refinance could allow you to pay off that debt with a mortgage loan that has an interest rate of 4% to 5%. This can significantly reduce your monthly payments and the overall amount of interest you'll need to pay over time.

Another benefit of a cash-out refinance is that it can simplify your debt repayment process by consolidating multiple debts into a single monthly mortgage payment. This can make it easier to keep track of your debt and stay on top of your payments. Additionally, by reducing the number of monthly payments you need to make, you can free up more of your monthly income to put towards your other financial goals, such as saving for retirement or building an emergency fund.

However, it's important to note that a cash-out refinance is not a one-size-fits-all solution, and it may not be the best option for everyone. Before considering a cash-out refinance, it's essential to assess your current financial situation, consider the costs associated with the refinance, and consult with a financial advisor or mortgage professional to determine if it's the right choice for you. Overall, a cash-out refinance can be a powerful tool to accelerate your journey towards becoming debt-free, but it's important to approach it with caution and careful consideration.

Before utilizing your home equity to pay off debt, it's important to carefully consider your options and consult with a financial professional. You should also make sure you understand the terms of any loan or line of credit you are considering, including the interest rate, fees, and repayment terms.

Pros and Cons of Using Home Equity for Debt Repayment

Pros:
- Lower interest rates: Home equity loans and HELOCs typically have lower interest rates than credit cards or other types of unsecured debt, which can save you money in interest charges.
- Consolidation: By using your home equity to pay off multiple debts, you can consolidate your debt and simplify your finances. This can make it easier to manage your payments and stay on top of your debt.
- Potential tax benefits: In some cases, the interest you pay on a home equity loan or HELOC may be tax-deductible. However, it's

important to consult with a tax professional to determine if you qualify for any tax benefits.

Cons:
- Risk of foreclosure: When you use your home equity as collateral for a loan or line of credit, you are putting your home at risk. If you are unable to make your payments, you could potentially lose your home to foreclosure.
- Fees: Home equity loans and HELOCs often come with fees such as application fees, appraisal fees, and closing costs. These fees can add up and make it more costly to access your home equity.
- Temptation to overspend: Accessing your home equity can provide

LESSON 5: STAYING ON TRACK AND MOTIVATED

Paying off debt can be a long and challenging process, but it's important to stay motivated and committed to achieving your goal of becoming debt-free. In this lesson, we will explore some tips for staying on track and motivated during the debt repayment process.

How to Stay Motivated During the Debt Repayment Process

1. Set realistic goals: Setting achievable goals can help you stay motivated and focused on your progress. Break down your debt repayment goal into smaller, more manageable goals, such as paying off a certain amount each month or paying off a specific debt.

2. Visualize your progress: Seeing your progress can be motivating and help you stay on track. Create a debt repayment tracker or chart to track your progress and visualize how far you've come.

3. Reward yourself: Celebrate your progress by rewarding yourself when you reach certain milestones. Treat yourself to a small indulgence or something you enjoy, like a night out or a movie.

4. Stay positive: Focus on the positive changes that come with reducing your debt, such as less stress and greater financial freedom. Surround yourself with positive people who support your goals and encourage you along the way.

Tips for Reducing Expenses and Increasing Income

1. Cut unnecessary expenses: Look for expenses that you can cut or reduce, such as subscription services or eating out. Consider making lifestyle changes, such as downsizing your home or car, to reduce your monthly expenses.

2. Increase your income: Look for ways to increase your income, such as taking on a side hustle, freelance work, or asking for a raise at work. Consider selling items you no longer need or use to generate extra cash.

3. Create a budget: Creating a budget can help you identify areas where you can cut expenses and prioritize your spending. Use tools like budgeting apps or spreadsheets to track your income and expenses.

4. Negotiate bills: Contact your service providers, such as your internet or cable company, to negotiate lower rates. You may be able to get a better deal by shopping around or threatening to switch providers.

How to Celebrate Your Progress and Stay Committed to Becoming Debt-Free

1. Reflect on your progress: Take time to reflect on your progress and how far you've come. Celebrate your milestones and give yourself credit for the hard work you've put in.

2. Share your progress: Share your progress with friends and family who will support and encourage you along the way. Join online communities or support groups to connect with others who are also working towards debt freedom.

3. Stay committed: Remember why you started and stay committed to your goal of becoming debt-free. Keep your goals in mind and stay focused on your progress, even when it's challenging.

4. Seek professional help: If you're struggling, consider seeking help from a financial professional or credit counselor. They can provide guidance and support to help you stay on track and achieve your debt repayment goals.

 A good loan officer can help because theyre used to assessing peoples financials. If you plan to accelerate your program using your homes equity that is important to review with them.

By staying motivated, reducing expenses, increasing income, and celebrating your progress, you can successfully pay off your debt and achieve financial freedom. Remember to stay committed to your goals and seek help when needed to stay on track.

LESSON 6: THE POWER OF PURPOSE IN BECOMING DEBT-FREE

Congratulations on coming this far in your journey towards financial freedom! You've learned valuable lessons about the snowball effect, assessing your current financial situation, creating a debt repayment plan, utilizing home equity to accelerate debt repayment, and staying motivated and on track. Now, it's time to explore how finding your purpose can be a powerful motivator in becoming debt-free.

A clear purpose can help you stay focused and motivated when the going gets tough. It provides a "why" behind your goal of becoming debt-free and can keep you on track when you're tempted to give up. In this chapter, we'll explore three areas where having a clear purpose can make a significant impact: family, children, and retirement.

Family

Your family is likely one of the most important things in your life. Becoming debt-free can help you provide for your loved ones and give them the life they deserve. Having a clear purpose for your family can help you stay motivated and focused on your goal. Maybe you want to save for a down payment on a house or take a family vacation. Whatever your purpose, keeping it in mind can help you stay on track and make the necessary sacrifices to achieve your goal.

Children

If you have children, becoming debt-free can have a significant impact on their lives. It can provide them with more opportunities and give them a solid financial foundation for their future. Maybe you want to save for their college education or help them start a business. Whatever your purpose, having a clear goal can help you stay motivated and make the necessary sacrifices to achieve it.

Retirement

Retirement may seem like a distant dream, but it's never too early to start planning for it. Becoming debt-free can help you save more for retirement and provide you with the financial security you need in your golden years. Having a clear purpose for your retirement can help you stay motivated and make the necessary sacrifices to achieve your goal. Maybe you want to retire early or travel the world. Whatever your purpose, keeping it in mind can help you stay on track and make the necessary sacrifices to achieve it.

Reduced stress and improved health

Becoming debt-free can also have a significant impact on your stress levels and overall health. Financial stress can take a toll on your mental and physical well-being, leading to anxiety, depression, and other health problems. By becoming debt-free, you can reduce your stress levels and improve your health, giving you the energy and motivation you need to achieve your goals.

In conclusion, finding your purpose can be a powerful motivator in becoming debt-free. By identifying your purpose in family, children, retirement, or other areas, you can stay motivated and focused on your goal. Remember, becoming debt-free is a marathon, not a sprint, but with a clear purpose and the right tools, you can achieve financial freedom and live the life you want..

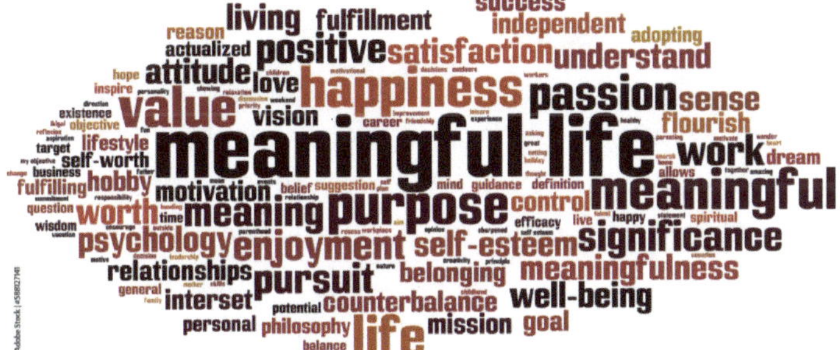

LESSON 7: IT'S A MARATHON NOT A SPRINT!

Congratulations on making it this far in your debt-free journey! You have learned valuable lessons about the snowball effect, assessing your current situation, creating a debt repayment plan, utilizing your home equity, staying on track and motivated, and finding your purpose. Now it is time to put it all together and implement the debt-free program.

The debt-free program is a one-day-at-a-time approach that requires patience and consistency. It is like running a marathon, where each step brings you closer to the finish line. The program is designed to help you become debt-free by following these steps:

Step 1: Start with the Snowball Effect

The snowball effect is a powerful tool that can help you pay off debt quickly. It involves paying off your smallest debt first, then using that money to pay off the next smallest debt, and so on. As you pay off each debt, you gain momentum and motivation to keep going.

Step 2: Assess Your Current Situation

Assessing your current situation involves taking a hard look at your debts, income, and expenses. You need to know how much you owe, how much you earn, and how much you spend each month. This information will help you create a debt repayment plan that works for you.

Step 3: Create a Debt Repayment Plan

Creating a debt repayment plan involves setting goals, prioritizing your debts, and figuring out how much you can afford to pay each month. You may need to make some sacrifices and cut back on expenses to free up more money for debt repayment. Remember, the more you can pay toward your debts, the faster you can become debt-free.

Step 4: Utilize Your Home Equity

If you own a home, you may be able to use your home equity to accelerate your debt repayment. This involves taking out a home equity loan or line of credit and using the funds to pay off high-interest debts. This can lower your interest rates and help you pay off your debts faster.

Step 5: Stay on Track and Motivated

Staying on track and motivated requires discipline and consistency. You need to stick to your debt repayment plan, track your progress, and celebrate your successes along the way. You may also need to find ways to stay motivated, such as reading personal finance blogs or listening to podcasts about debt-free living.

Step 6: Find Your Purpose

Finding your purpose involves figuring out why you want to become debt-free. Maybe you want to be able to save for retirement, travel the world, or start your own business. Whatever your purpose is, it can help you stay motivated and focused on your goal.

Remember, becoming debt-free is a marathon, not a sprint. It takes time, patience, and perseverance. But with the right mindset and tools, you can achieve financial freedom and live the life you want. Start your debt-free program today and take the first step toward a debt-free future.

DEBT TRACKER WORKSHEET

Use this worksheet to track your debt and monitor your progress towards becoming debt-free.

 Just writing it down helps you understand where you stand. If you don't want to use this. Search the internet for one you like. BUT **WRITE IT DOWN!!**

Debt Name: _______________________________

Current Balance: _______________________________

Interest Rate: _______________________________

Minimum Payment: _______________________________

Monthly Payment: _______________________________

Target Payoff Date: _______________________________

```
Month/Year | Balance | Payment | Interest | Principal | New Balance
-----------|--------|---------|---------|----------|------------
MM/YYYY | $XXXXX | $XXXXX | $XXXXX | $XXXXX | $XXXXX
MM/YYYY | $XXXXX | $XXXXX | $XXXXX | $XXXXX | $XXXXX
```

Instructions:

1. Fill in the debt name, current balance, interest rate, minimum payment, monthly payment, and target payoff date for each debt you want to track.

2. Each month, record the balance, payment, interest, principal, and new balance for each debt.

3. Use the table to monitor your progress towards paying off each debt and becoming debt-free.

4. Update the table regularly to stay on top of your progress and adjust your payment strategy as needed.

Tips:

1. Prioritize paying off debts with higher interest rates first.

2. Consider consolidating high-interest debt with a lower-interest loan or line of credit.

3. Increase your monthly payments when possible to pay off debt faster.

4. Celebrate your progress along the way to stay motivated and committed to becoming debt-free.